This Journal

BELONGS TO

_____

_____

Dedication

This Restaurant Review Journal is dedicated to all the people out there who love to track their Restaurant Reviews and document their findings in the process.

You are my inspiration for producing books and I'm honored to be a part of keeping all of your Restaurant notes, and records organized.

This journal notebook will help you record your details about tracking your dining out experiences.

Thoughtfully put together with these sections to record: Restaurant Name, Party Members, Service, Beverage Service, Cleanliness, Overall Review, Impressions, Mileage, & Compensation Received.

How to Use this Book

The purpose of this book is to keep all of your Restaurant Review notes all in one place. It will help keep you organized.

This Restaurant Journal Book will allow you to accurately document every detail about all of your dining out experiences. It's a great way to chart your course through Restaurant Reviewing.

Here are examples of the prompts for you to fill in and write about your experience in this book:

1. Restaurant Name- Restaurant Name, Date of Visit, Time of Reservation, Server Name, Manager on Duty

2. Party Members - Names, Meals Ordered, Quality, Price

3. Service - Warm Welcome?, Attentiveness & Pace of Service, Gave Good Recommendations?, Accuracy of Service.

4. Beverage Service - Good Recommendations?, Experience Details?

5. Cleanliness - Restaurant Cleanliness, Restroom Cleanliness

6. Overall Review & Impressions - Would You Recommend?, Opportunities for Improvement.

7. Mileage, Compensation, Received - Blank Lined to Write Your Number

Restaurant _____ Date of visit _____ Time _____

Server name _____ Manager on duty _____

Party member	Meal ordered	Quality	Price
		Total	

Server

Warm welcome? _____

Attentiveness and pace of service _____

Gave good recommendations? _____

Accuracy of service _____

Beverage Service

Good recommendations? _____ Checked ID? _____

Experience? _____ Quality of drinks _____

Restaurant

Restaurant cleanliness _____

Restroom cleanliness _____

Overall Impressions

Would you recommend this restaurant? _____

Opportunities for improvement _____

Mileage _____ Compensation _____ Received _____

Restaurant _____ Date of visit _____ Time _____

Server name _____ Manager on duty _____

Party member	Meal ordered	Quality	Price
		Total	

Server

Warm welcome? _____

Attentiveness and pace of service _____

Gave good recommendations? _____

Accuracy of service _____

Beverage Service

Good recommendations? _____   Checked ID? _____

Experience? _____   Quality of drinks _____

Restaurant

Restaurant cleanliness _____

Restroom cleanliness _____

Overall Impressions

Would you recommend this restaurant? _____

Opportunities for improvement _____

Mileage _____   Compensation _____   Received _____

Restaurant _____ Date of visit _____ Time _____

Server name _____ Manager on duty _____

Party member	Meal ordered	Quality	Price
		Total	

Server

Warm welcome? _____

Attentiveness and pace of service _____

Gave good recommendations? _____

Accuracy of service _____

Beverage Service

Good recommendations? _____ Checked ID? _____

Experience? _____ Quality of drinks _____

Restaurant

Restaurant cleanliness _____

Restroom cleanliness _____

Overall Impressions

Would you recommend this restaurant? _____

Opportunities for improvement _____

Mileage _____ Compensation _____ Received _____

Restaurant _____   Date of visit _____   Time _____

Server name _____   Manager on duty _____

Party member	Meal ordered	Quality	Price
		Total	

Server

Warm welcome? _____

Attentiveness and pace of service _____

Gave good recommendations? _____

Accuracy of service _____

Beverage Service

Good recommendations? _____   Checked ID? _____

Experience? _____   Quality of drinks _____

Restaurant

Restaurant cleanliness _____

Restroom cleanliness _____

Overall Impressions

Would you recommend this restaurant? _____

Opportunities for improvement _____

Mileage _____   Compensation _____   Received _____

Restaurant _____ Date of visit _____ Time _____

Server name _____ Manager on duty _____

Party member	Meal ordered	Quality	Price
		Total	

Server

Warm welcome? _____

Attentiveness and pace of service _____

Gave good recommendations? _____

Accuracy of service _____

Beverage Service

Good recommendations? _____ Checked ID? _____

Experience? _____ Quality of drinks _____

Restaurant

Restaurant cleanliness _____

Restroom cleanliness _____

Overall Impressions

Would you recommend this restaurant? _____

Opportunities for improvement _____

Mileage _____ Compensation _____ Received _____

Restaurant _____   Date of visit _____   Time _____

Server name _____   Manager on duty _____

Party member	Meal ordered	Quality	Price
		Total	

Server

Warm welcome? _____

Attentiveness and pace of service _____

Gave good recommendations? _____

Accuracy of service _____

Beverage Service

Good recommendations? _____   Checked ID? _____

Experience? _____   Quality of drinks _____

Restaurant

Restaurant cleanliness _____

Restroom cleanliness _____

Overall Impressions

Would you recommend this restaurant? _____

Opportunities for improvement _____

Mileage _____   Compensation _____   Received _____

Restaurant _____ Date of visit _____ Time _____

Server name _____ Manager on duty _____

Party member	Meal ordered	Quality	Price
		Total	

Server

Warm welcome? _____

Attentiveness and pace of service _____

Gave good recommendations? _____

Accuracy of service _____

Beverage Service

Good recommendations? _____ Checked ID? _____

Experience? _____ Quality of drinks _____

Restaurant

Restaurant cleanliness _____

Restroom cleanliness _____

Overall Impressions

Would you recommend this restaurant? _____

Opportunities for improvement _____

Mileage _____ Compensation _____ Received _____

Restaurant _____ Date of visit _____ Time _____

Server name _____ Manager on duty _____

Party member	Meal ordered	Quality	Price
		Total	

Server

Warm welcome? _____

Attentiveness and pace of service _____

Gave good recommendations? _____

Accuracy of service _____

Beverage Service

Good recommendations? _____ Checked ID? _____

Experience? _____ Quality of drinks _____

Restaurant

Restaurant cleanliness _____

Restroom cleanliness _____

Overall Impressions

Would you recommend this restaurant? _____

Opportunities for improvement _____

Mileage _____ Compensation _____ Received _____

Restaurant _____ Date of visit _____ Time _____

Server name _____ Manager on duty _____

Party member	Meal ordered	Quality	Price
		Total	

Server

Warm welcome? _____

Attentiveness and pace of service _____

Gave good recommendations? _____

Accuracy of service _____

Beverage Service

Good recommendations? _____   Checked ID? _____

Experience? _____   Quality of drinks _____

Restaurant

Restaurant cleanliness _____

Restroom cleanliness _____

Overall Impressions

Would you recommend this restaurant? _____

Opportunities for improvement _____

Mileage _____ Compensation _____ Received _____

Restaurant _____ Date of visit _____ Time _____

Server name _____ Manager on duty _____

Party member	Meal ordered	Quality	Price
		Total	

Server

Warm welcome? _____

Attentiveness and pace of service _____

Gave good recommendations? _____

Accuracy of service _____

Beverage Service

Good recommendations? _____ Checked ID? _____

Experience? _____ Quality of drinks _____

Restaurant

Restaurant cleanliness _____

Restroom cleanliness _____

Overall Impressions

Would you recommend this restaurant? _____

Opportunities for improvement _____

Mileage _____ Compensation _____ Received _____

Restaurant _____ Date of visit _____ Time _____

Server name _____ Manager on duty _____

Party member	Meal ordered	Quality	Price
		Total	

Server

Warm welcome? _____

Attentiveness and pace of service _____

Gave good recommendations? _____

Accuracy of service _____

Beverage Service

Good recommendations? _____ Checked ID? _____

Experience? _____ Quality of drinks _____

Restaurant

Restaurant cleanliness _____

Restroom cleanliness _____

Overall Impressions

Would you recommend this restaurant? _____

Opportunities for improvement _____

Mileage _____ Compensation _____ Received _____

Restaurant _____   Date of visit _____   Time _____

Server name _____   Manager on duty _____

Party member	Meal ordered	Quality	Price
		Total	

Server

Warm welcome? _____

Attentiveness and pace of service _____

Gave good recommendations? _____

Accuracy of service _____

Beverage Service

Good recommendations? _____   Checked ID? _____

Experience? _____   Quality of drinks _____

Restaurant

Restaurant cleanliness _____

Restroom cleanliness _____

Overall Impressions

Would you recommend this restaurant? _____

Opportunities for improvement _____

Mileage _____   Compensation _____   Received _____

Restaurant _____ Date of visit _____ Time _____

Server name _____ Manager on duty _____

Party member	Meal ordered	Quality	Price
		Total	

Server

Warm welcome? _____

Attentiveness and pace of service _____

Gave good recommendations? _____

Accuracy of service _____

Beverage Service

Good recommendations? _____   Checked ID? _____

Experience? _____   Quality of drinks _____

Restaurant

Restaurant cleanliness _____

Restroom cleanliness _____

Overall Impressions

Would you recommend this restaurant? _____

Opportunities for improvement _____

Mileage _____   Compensation _____   Received _____

Restaurant _____ Date of visit _____ Time _____

Server name _____ Manager on duty _____

Party member	Meal ordered	Quality	Price
		Total	

Server

Warm welcome? _____

Attentiveness and pace of service _____

Gave good recommendations? _____

Accuracy of service _____

Beverage Service

Good recommendations? _____ Checked ID? _____

Experience? _____ Quality of drinks _____

Restaurant

Restaurant cleanliness _____

Restroom cleanliness _____

Overall Impressions

Would you recommend this restaurant? _____

Opportunities for improvement _____

Mileage _____ Compensation _____ Received _____

Restaurant _____ Date of visit _____ Time _____

Server name _____ Manager on duty _____

Party member	Meal ordered	Quality	Price
		Total	

Server

Warm welcome? _____

Attentiveness and pace of service _____

Gave good recommendations? _____

Accuracy of service _____

Beverage Service

Good recommendations? _____ Checked ID? _____

Experience? _____ Quality of drinks _____

Restaurant

Restaurant cleanliness _____

Restroom cleanliness _____

Overall Impressions

Would you recommend this restaurant? _____

Opportunities for improvement _____

Mileage _____ Compensation _____ Received _____

Restaurant _____ Date of visit _____ Time _____

Server name _____ Manager on duty _____

Party member	Meal ordered	Quality	Price
		Total	

Server

Warm welcome? _____

Attentiveness and pace of service _____

Gave good recommendations? _____

Accuracy of service _____

Beverage Service

Good recommendations? _____ Checked ID? _____

Experience? _____ Quality of drinks _____

Restaurant

Restaurant cleanliness _____

Restroom cleanliness _____

Overall Impressions

Would you recommend this restaurant? _____

Opportunities for improvement _____

Mileage _____ Compensation _____ Received _____

Restaurant _____ Date of visit _____ Time _____

Server name _____ Manager on duty _____

Party member	Meal ordered	Quality	Price
		Total	

Server

Warm welcome? _____

Attentiveness and pace of service _____

Gave good recommendations? _____

Accuracy of service _____

Beverage Service

Good recommendations? _____ Checked ID? _____

Experience? _____ Quality of drinks _____

Restaurant

Restaurant cleanliness _____

Restroom cleanliness _____

Overall Impressions

Would you recommend this restaurant? _____

Opportunities for improvement _____

Mileage _____ Compensation _____ Received _____

Restaurant _____ Date of visit _____ Time _____

Server name _____ Manager on duty _____

Party member	Meal ordered	Quality	Price
		Total	

Server

Warm welcome? _____

Attentiveness and pace of service _____

Gave good recommendations? _____

Accuracy of service _____

Beverage Service

Good recommendations? _____ Checked ID? _____

Experience? _____ Quality of drinks _____

Restaurant

Restaurant cleanliness _____

Restroom cleanliness _____

Overall Impressions

Would you recommend this restaurant? _____

Opportunities for improvement _____

Mileage _____ Compensation _____ Received _____

Restaurant _____ Date of visit _____ Time _____

Server name _____ Manager on duty _____

Party member	Meal ordered	Quality	Price
		Total	

Server

Warm welcome? _____

Attentiveness and pace of service _____

Gave good recommendations? _____

Accuracy of service _____

Beverage Service

Good recommendations? _____ Checked ID? _____

Experience? _____ Quality of drinks _____

Restaurant

Restaurant cleanliness _____

Restroom cleanliness _____

Overall Impressions

Would you recommend this restaurant? _____

Opportunities for improvement _____

Mileage _____ Compensation _____ Received _____

Restaurant _____ Date of visit _____ Time _____

Server name _____ Manager on duty _____

Party member	Meal ordered	Quality	Price
		Total	

Server

Warm welcome? _____

Attentiveness and pace of service _____

Gave good recommendations? _____

Accuracy of service _____

Beverage Service

Good recommendations? _____ Checked ID? _____

Experience? _____ Quality of drinks _____

Restaurant

Restaurant cleanliness _____

Restroom cleanliness _____

Overall Impressions

Would you recommend this restaurant? _____

Opportunities for improvement _____

Mileage _____ Compensation _____ Received _____

Restaurant _____ Date of visit _____ Time _____

Server name _____ Manager on duty _____

Party member	Meal ordered	Quality	Price
		Total	

Server

Warm welcome? _____

Attentiveness and pace of service _____

Gave good recommendations? _____

Accuracy of service _____

Beverage Service

Good recommendations? _____ Checked ID? _____

Experience? _____ Quality of drinks _____

Restaurant

Restaurant cleanliness _____

Restroom cleanliness _____

Overall Impressions

Would you recommend this restaurant? _____

Opportunities for improvement _____

Mileage _____ Compensation _____ Received _____

Restaurant _____ Date of visit _____ Time _____

Server name _____ Manager on duty _____

Party member	Meal ordered	Quality	Price
		Total	

Server

Warm welcome? _____

Attentiveness and pace of service _____

Gave good recommendations? _____

Accuracy of service _____

Beverage Service

Good recommendations? _____ Checked ID? _____

Experience? _____ Quality of drinks _____

Restaurant

Restaurant cleanliness _____

Restroom cleanliness _____

Overall Impressions

Would you recommend this restaurant? _____

Opportunities for improvement _____

Mileage _____ Compensation _____ Received _____

Restaurant _____ Date of visit _____ Time _____

Server name _____ Manager on duty _____

Party member	Meal ordered	Quality	Price
		Total	

Server

Warm welcome? _____

Attentiveness and pace of service _____

Gave good recommendations? _____

Accuracy of service _____

Beverage Service

Good recommendations? _____ Checked ID? _____

Experience? _____ Quality of drinks _____

Restaurant

Restaurant cleanliness _____

Restroom cleanliness _____

Overall Impressions

Would you recommend this restaurant? _____

Opportunities for improvement _____

Mileage _____ Compensation _____ Received _____

Restaurant _____   Date of visit _____   Time _____

Server name _____   Manager on duty _____

Party member	Meal ordered	Quality	Price
		Total	

Server

Warm welcome? _____

Attentiveness and pace of service _____

Gave good recommendations? _____

Accuracy of service _____

Beverage Service

Good recommendations? _____   Checked ID? _____

Experience? _____   Quality of drinks _____

Restaurant

Restaurant cleanliness _____

Restroom cleanliness _____

Overall Impressions

Would you recommend this restaurant? _____

Opportunities for improvement _____

Mileage _____   Compensation _____   Received _____

Restaurant _____ Date of visit _____ Time _____

Server name _____ Manager on duty _____

Party member	Meal ordered	Quality	Price
		Total	

Server

Warm welcome? _____

Attentiveness and pace of service _____

Gave good recommendations? _____

Accuracy of service _____

Beverage Service

Good recommendations? _____ Checked ID? _____

Experience? _____ Quality of drinks _____

Restaurant

Restaurant cleanliness _____

Restroom cleanliness _____

Overall Impressions

Would you recommend this restaurant? _____

Opportunities for improvement _____

Mileage _____ Compensation _____ Received _____

Restaurant _____ Date of visit _____ Time _____

Server name _____ Manager on duty _____

Party member	Meal ordered	Quality	Price
		Total	

Server

Warm welcome? _____

Attentiveness and pace of service _____

Gave good recommendations? _____

Accuracy of service _____

Beverage Service

Good recommendations? _____ Checked ID? _____

Experience? _____ Quality of drinks _____

Restaurant

Restaurant cleanliness _____

Restroom cleanliness _____

Overall Impressions

Would you recommend this restaurant? _____

Opportunities for improvement _____

Mileage _____ Compensation _____ Received _____

Restaurant _____   Date of visit _____   Time _____

Server name _____   Manager on duty _____

Party member	Meal ordered	Quality	Price
		Total	

Server

Warm welcome? _____

Attentiveness and pace of service _____

Gave good recommendations? _____

Accuracy of service _____

Beverage Service

Good recommendations? _____   Checked ID? _____

Experience? _____   Quality of drinks _____

Restaurant

Restaurant cleanliness _____

Restroom cleanliness _____

Overall Impressions

Would you recommend this restaurant? _____

Opportunities for improvement _____

Mileage _____   Compensation _____   Received _____

Restaurant _____   Date of visit _____   Time _____

Server name _____   Manager on duty _____

Party member	Meal ordered	Quality	Price
		Total	

Server

Warm welcome? _____

Attentiveness and pace of service _____

Gave good recommendations? _____

Accuracy of service _____

Beverage Service

Good recommendations? _____   Checked ID? _____

Experience? _____   Quality of drinks _____

Restaurant

Restaurant cleanliness _____

Restroom cleanliness _____

Overall Impressions

Would you recommend this restaurant? _____

Opportunities for improvement _____

Mileage _____   Compensation _____   Received _____

| Restaurant | _____ | Date of visit | _____ | Time | _____ |

Server name _____   Manager on duty _____

Party member	Meal ordered	Quality	Price
		Total	

Server

Warm welcome? _____

Attentiveness and pace of service _____

Gave good recommendations? _____

Accuracy of service _____

Beverage Service

Good recommendations? _____   Checked ID? _____

Experience? _____   Quality of drinks _____

Restaurant

Restaurant cleanliness _____

Restroom cleanliness _____

Overall Impressions

Would you recommend this restaurant? _____

Opportunities for improvement _____

Mileage _____   Compensation _____   Received _____

Restaurant _____ Date of visit _____ Time _____

Server name _____ Manager on duty _____

Party member	Meal ordered	Quality	Price
		Total	

Server

Warm welcome? _____

Attentiveness and pace of service _____

Gave good recommendations? _____

Accuracy of service _____

Beverage Service

Good recommendations? _____   Checked ID? _____

Experience? _____   Quality of drinks _____

Restaurant

Restaurant cleanliness _____

Restroom cleanliness _____

Overall Impressions

Would you recommend this restaurant? _____

Opportunities for improvement _____

Mileage _____ Compensation _____ Received _____

Restaurant _____ Date of visit _____ Time _____

Server name _____ Manager on duty _____

Party member	Meal ordered	Quality	Price
		Total	

Server

Warm welcome? _____

Attentiveness and pace of service _____

Gave good recommendations? _____

Accuracy of service _____

Beverage Service

Good recommendations? _____ Checked ID? _____

Experience? _____ Quality of drinks _____

Restaurant

Restaurant cleanliness _____

Restroom cleanliness _____

Overall Impressions

Would you recommend this restaurant? _____

Opportunities for improvement _____

Mileage _____ Compensation _____ Received _____

Restaurant _____ Date of visit _____ Time _____

Server name _____ Manager on duty _____

Party member	Meal ordered	Quality	Price
		Total	

Server

Warm welcome? _____

Attentiveness and pace of service _____

Gave good recommendations? _____

Accuracy of service _____

Beverage Service

Good recommendations? _____ Checked ID? _____

Experience? _____ Quality of drinks _____

Restaurant

Restaurant cleanliness _____

Restroom cleanliness _____

Overall Impressions

Would you recommend this restaurant? _____

Opportunities for improvement _____

Mileage _____ Compensation _____ Received _____

Restaurant _____ Date of visit _____ Time _____

Server name _____ Manager on duty _____

Party member	Meal ordered	Quality	Price
		Total	

Server

Warm welcome? _____

Attentiveness and pace of service _____

Gave good recommendations? _____

Accuracy of service _____

Beverage Service

Good recommendations? _____ Checked ID? _____

Experience? _____ Quality of drinks _____

Restaurant

Restaurant cleanliness _____

Restroom cleanliness _____

Overall Impressions

Would you recommend this restaurant? _____

Opportunities for improvement _____

Mileage _____ Compensation _____ Received _____

Restaurant _____ Date of visit _____ Time _____

Server name _____ Manager on duty _____

Party member	Meal ordered	Quality	Price
		Total	

Server

Warm welcome? _____

Attentiveness and pace of service _____

Gave good recommendations? _____

Accuracy of service _____

Beverage Service

Good recommendations? _____ Checked ID? _____

Experience? _____ Quality of drinks _____

Restaurant

Restaurant cleanliness _____

Restroom cleanliness _____

Overall Impressions

Would you recommend this restaurant? _____

Opportunities for improvement _____

Mileage _____ Compensation _____ Received _____

Restaurant _____ Date of visit _____ Time _____

Server name _____ Manager on duty _____

Party member	Meal ordered	Quality	Price
	Total		

Server

Warm welcome? _____

Attentiveness and pace of service _____

Gave good recommendations? _____

Accuracy of service _____

Beverage Service

Good recommendations? _____ Checked ID? _____

Experience? _____ Quality of drinks _____

Restaurant

Restaurant cleanliness _____

Restroom cleanliness _____

Overall Impressions

Would you recommend this restaurant? _____

Opportunities for improvement _____

Mileage _____ Compensation _____ Received _____

Restaurant _____ Date of visit _____ Time _____

Server name _____ Manager on duty _____

Party member	Meal ordered	Quality	Price
		Total	

Server

Warm welcome? _____

Attentiveness and pace of service _____

Gave good recommendations? _____

Accuracy of service _____

Beverage Service

Good recommendations? _____ Checked ID? _____

Experience? _____ Quality of drinks _____

Restaurant

Restaurant cleanliness _____

Restroom cleanliness _____

Overall Impressions

Would you recommend this restaurant? _____

Opportunities for improvement _____

Mileage _____ Compensation _____ Received _____

Restaurant _____ Date of visit _____ Time _____

Server name _____ Manager on duty _____

Party member	Meal ordered	Quality	Price
		Total	

Server

Warm welcome? _____

Attentiveness and pace of service _____

Gave good recommendations? _____

Accuracy of service _____

Beverage Service

Good recommendations? _____ Checked ID? _____

Experience? _____ Quality of drinks _____

Restaurant

Restaurant cleanliness _____

Restroom cleanliness _____

Overall Impressions

Would you recommend this restaurant? _____

Opportunities for improvement _____

Mileage _____ Compensation _____ Received _____

Restaurant _____   Date of visit _____   Time _____

Server name _____   Manager on duty _____

Party member	Meal ordered	Quality	Price
		Total	

Server

Warm welcome? _____

Attentiveness and pace of service _____

Gave good recommendations? _____

Accuracy of service _____

Beverage Service

Good recommendations? _____   Checked ID? _____

Experience? _____   Quality of drinks _____

Restaurant

Restaurant cleanliness _____

Restroom cleanliness _____

Overall Impressions

Would you recommend this restaurant? _____

Opportunities for improvement _____

Mileage _____   Compensation _____   Received _____

Restaurant _____ Date of visit _____ Time _____

Server name _____ Manager on duty _____

Party member	Meal ordered	Quality	Price
		Total	

Server

Warm welcome? _____

Attentiveness and pace of service _____

Gave good recommendations? _____

Accuracy of service _____

Beverage Service

Good recommendations? _____ Checked ID? _____

Experience? _____ Quality of drinks _____

Restaurant

Restaurant cleanliness _____

Restroom cleanliness _____

Overall Impressions

Would you recommend this restaurant? _____

Opportunities for improvement _____

Mileage _____ Compensation _____ Received _____

Restaurant _____ Date of visit _____ Time _____

Server name _____ Manager on duty _____

Party member	Meal ordered	Quality	Price
		Total	

Server

Warm welcome? _____

Attentiveness and pace of service _____

Gave good recommendations? _____

Accuracy of service _____

Beverage Service

Good recommendations? _____ Checked ID? _____

Experience? _____ Quality of drinks _____

Restaurant

Restaurant cleanliness _____

Restroom cleanliness _____

Overall Impressions

Would you recommend this restaurant? _____

Opportunities for improvement _____

Mileage _____ Compensation _____ Received _____

Restaurant _____ Date of visit _____ Time _____

Server name _____ Manager on duty _____

Party member	Meal ordered	Quality	Price
		Total	

Server

Warm welcome? _____

Attentiveness and pace of service _____

Gave good recommendations? _____

Accuracy of service _____

Beverage Service

Good recommendations? _____   Checked ID? _____

Experience? _____   Quality of drinks _____

Restaurant

Restaurant cleanliness _____

Restroom cleanliness _____

Overall Impressions

Would you recommend this restaurant? _____

Opportunities for improvement _____

Mileage _____   Compensation _____   Received _____

Restaurant _____ Date of visit _____ Time _____

Server name _____ Manager on duty _____

Party member	Meal ordered	Quality	Price
		Total	

Server

Warm welcome? _____

Attentiveness and pace of service _____

Gave good recommendations? _____

Accuracy of service _____

Beverage Service

Good recommendations? _____ Checked ID? _____

Experience? _____ Quality of drinks _____

Restaurant

Restaurant cleanliness _____

Restroom cleanliness _____

Overall Impressions

Would you recommend this restaurant? _____

Opportunities for improvement _____

Mileage _____ Compensation _____ Received _____

Restaurant _____ Date of visit _____ Time _____

Server name _____ Manager on duty _____

Party member	Meal ordered	Quality	Price
		Total	

Server

Warm welcome? _____

Attentiveness and pace of service _____

Gave good recommendations? _____

Accuracy of service _____

Beverage Service

Good recommendations? _____ Checked ID? _____

Experience? _____ Quality of drinks _____

Restaurant

Restaurant cleanliness _____

Restroom cleanliness _____

Overall Impressions

Would you recommend this restaurant? _____

Opportunities for improvement _____

Mileage _____ Compensation _____ Received _____

Restaurant _____ Date of visit _____ Time _____

Server name _____ Manager on duty _____

Party member	Meal ordered	Quality	Price
		Total	

Server

Warm welcome? _____

Attentiveness and pace of service _____

Gave good recommendations? _____

Accuracy of service _____

Beverage Service

Good recommendations? _____ Checked ID? _____

Experience? _____ Quality of drinks _____

Restaurant

Restaurant cleanliness _____

Restroom cleanliness _____

Overall Impressions

Would you recommend this restaurant? _____

Opportunities for improvement _____

Mileage _____ Compensation _____ Received _____

Restaurant _____ Date of visit _____ Time _____

Server name _____ Manager on duty _____

Party member	Meal ordered	Quality	Price
		Total	

Server

Warm welcome? _____

Attentiveness and pace of service _____

Gave good recommendations? _____

Accuracy of service _____

Beverage Service

Good recommendations? _____ Checked ID? _____

Experience? _____ Quality of drinks _____

Restaurant

Restaurant cleanliness _____

Restroom cleanliness _____

Overall Impressions

Would you recommend this restaurant? _____

Opportunities for improvement _____

Mileage _____ Compensation _____ Received _____

Restaurant _____ Date of visit _____ Time _____

Server name _____ Manager on duty _____

Party member	Meal ordered	Quality	Price
		Total	

Server

Warm welcome? _____

Attentiveness and pace of service _____

Gave good recommendations? _____

Accuracy of service _____

Beverage Service

Good recommendations? _____ Checked ID? _____

Experience? _____ Quality of drinks _____

Restaurant

Restaurant cleanliness _____

Restroom cleanliness _____

Overall Impressions

Would you recommend this restaurant? _____

Opportunities for improvement _____

Mileage _____ Compensation _____ Received _____

Restaurant _____ Date of visit _____ Time _____

Server name _____ Manager on duty _____

Party member	Meal ordered	Quality	Price
		Total	

Server

Warm welcome? _____

Attentiveness and pace of service _____

Gave good recommendations? _____

Accuracy of service _____

Beverage Service

Good recommendations? _____ Checked ID? _____

Experience? _____ Quality of drinks _____

Restaurant

Restaurant cleanliness _____

Restroom cleanliness _____

Overall Impressions

Would you recommend this restaurant? _____

Opportunities for improvement _____

Mileage _____ Compensation _____ Received _____

Restaurant _____ Date of visit _____ Time _____

Server name _____ Manager on duty _____

Party member	Meal ordered	Quality	Price
		Total	

Server

Warm welcome? _____

Attentiveness and pace of service _____

Gave good recommendations? _____

Accuracy of service _____

Beverage Service

Good recommendations? _____ Checked ID? _____

Experience? _____ Quality of drinks _____

Restaurant

Restaurant cleanliness _____

Restroom cleanliness _____

Overall Impressions

Would you recommend this restaurant? _____

Opportunities for improvement _____

Mileage _____ Compensation _____ Received _____

Restaurant _____ Date of visit _____ Time _____

Server name _____ Manager on duty _____

Party member	Meal ordered	Quality	Price
		Total	

Server

Warm welcome? _____

Attentiveness and pace of service _____

Gave good recommendations? _____

Accuracy of service _____

Beverage Service

Good recommendations? _____ Checked ID? _____

Experience? _____ Quality of drinks _____

Restaurant

Restaurant cleanliness _____

Restroom cleanliness _____

Overall Impressions

Would you recommend this restaurant? _____

Opportunities for improvement _____

Mileage _____ Compensation _____ Received _____

Restaurant _____   Date of visit _____   Time _____

Server name _____   Manager on duty _____

Party member	Meal ordered	Quality	Price
		Total	

Server

Warm welcome? _____

Attentiveness and pace of service _____

Gave good recommendations? _____

Accuracy of service _____

Beverage Service

Good recommendations? _____   Checked ID? _____

Experience? _____   Quality of drinks _____

Restaurant

Restaurant cleanliness _____

Restroom cleanliness _____

Overall Impressions

Would you recommend this restaurant? _____

Opportunities for improvement _____

Mileage _____   Compensation _____   Received _____

Restaurant _____ Date of visit _____ Time _____

Server name _____ Manager on duty _____

Party member	Meal ordered	Quality	Price
		Total	

Server

Warm welcome? _____

Attentiveness and pace of service _____

Gave good recommendations? _____

Accuracy of service _____

Beverage Service

Good recommendations? _____ Checked ID? _____

Experience? _____ Quality of drinks _____

Restaurant

Restaurant cleanliness _____

Restroom cleanliness _____

Overall Impressions

Would you recommend this restaurant? _____

Opportunities for improvement _____

Mileage _____ Compensation _____ Received _____

Restaurant _____ Date of visit _____ Time _____

Server name _____ Manager on duty _____

Party member	Meal ordered	Quality	Price
		Total	

Server

Warm welcome? _____

Attentiveness and pace of service _____

Gave good recommendations? _____

Accuracy of service _____

Beverage Service

Good recommendations? _____ Checked ID? _____

Experience? _____ Quality of drinks _____

Restaurant

Restaurant cleanliness _____

Restroom cleanliness _____

Overall Impressions

Would you recommend this restaurant? _____

Opportunities for improvement _____

Mileage _____ Compensation _____ Received _____

Restaurant _____   Date of visit _____   Time _____

Server name _____   Manager on duty _____

Party member	Meal ordered	Quality	Price
		Total	

Server

Warm welcome? _____

Attentiveness and pace of service _____

Gave good recommendations? _____

Accuracy of service _____

Beverage Service

Good recommendations? _____   Checked ID? _____

Experience? _____   Quality of drinks _____

Restaurant

Restaurant cleanliness _____

Restroom cleanliness _____

Overall Impressions

Would you recommend this restaurant? _____

Opportunities for improvement _____

Mileage _____   Compensation _____   Received _____

Restaurant _____ Date of visit _____ Time _____

Server name _____ Manager on duty _____

Party member	Meal ordered	Quality	Price
		Total	

Server

Warm welcome? _____

Attentiveness and pace of service _____

Gave good recommendations? _____

Accuracy of service _____

Beverage Service

Good recommendations? _____ Checked ID? _____

Experience? _____ Quality of drinks _____

Restaurant

Restaurant cleanliness _____

Restroom cleanliness _____

Overall Impressions

Would you recommend this restaurant? _____

Opportunities for improvement _____

Mileage _____ Compensation _____ Received _____

Restaurant _____ Date of visit _____ Time _____

Server name _____ Manager on duty _____

Party member	Meal ordered	Quality	Price
		Total	

Server

Warm welcome? _____

Attentiveness and pace of service _____

Gave good recommendations? _____

Accuracy of service _____

Beverage Service

Good recommendations? _____ Checked ID? _____

Experience? _____ Quality of drinks _____

Restaurant

Restaurant cleanliness _____

Restroom cleanliness _____

Overall Impressions

Would you recommend this restaurant? _____

Opportunities for improvement _____

Mileage _____ Compensation _____ Received _____

Restaurant _____ Date of visit _____ Time _____

Server name _____ Manager on duty _____

Party member	Meal ordered	Quality	Price
		Total	

Server

Warm welcome? _____

Attentiveness and pace of service _____

Gave good recommendations? _____

Accuracy of service _____

Beverage Service

Good recommendations? _____ Checked ID? _____

Experience? _____ Quality of drinks _____

Restaurant

Restaurant cleanliness _____

Restroom cleanliness _____

Overall Impressions

Would you recommend this restaurant? _____

Opportunities for improvement _____

Mileage _____ Compensation _____ Received _____

Restaurant _____ Date of visit _____ Time _____

Server name _____ Manager on duty _____

Party member	Meal ordered	Quality	Price
		Total	

Server

Warm welcome? _____

Attentiveness and pace of service _____

Gave good recommendations? _____

Accuracy of service _____

Beverage Service

Good recommendations? _____ Checked ID? _____

Experience? _____ Quality of drinks _____

Restaurant

Restaurant cleanliness _____

Restroom cleanliness _____

Overall Impressions

Would you recommend this restaurant? _____

Opportunities for improvement _____

Mileage _____ Compensation _____ Received _____

Restaurant _____ Date of visit _____ Time _____

Server name _____ Manager on duty _____

Party member	Meal ordered	Quality	Price
		Total	

Server

Warm welcome? _____

Attentiveness and pace of service _____

Gave good recommendations? _____

Accuracy of service _____

Beverage Service

Good recommendations? _____ Checked ID? _____

Experience? _____ Quality of drinks _____

Restaurant

Restaurant cleanliness _____

Restroom cleanliness _____

Overall Impressions

Would you recommend this restaurant? _____

Opportunities for improvement _____

Mileage _____ Compensation _____ Received _____

Restaurant _____ Date of visit _____ Time _____

Server name _____ Manager on duty _____

Party member	Meal ordered	Quality	Price
		Total	

Server

Warm welcome? _____

Attentiveness and pace of service _____

Gave good recommendations? _____

Accuracy of service _____

Beverage Service

Good recommendations? _____ Checked ID? _____

Experience? _____ Quality of drinks _____

Restaurant

Restaurant cleanliness _____

Restroom cleanliness _____

Overall Impressions

Would you recommend this restaurant? _____

Opportunities for improvement _____

Mileage _____ Compensation _____ Received _____

Restaurant _____ Date of visit _____ Time _____

Server name _____ Manager on duty _____

Party member	Meal ordered	Quality	Price
		Total	

Server

Warm welcome? _____

Attentiveness and pace of service _____

Gave good recommendations? _____

Accuracy of service _____

Beverage Service

Good recommendations? _____ Checked ID? _____

Experience? _____ Quality of drinks _____

Restaurant

Restaurant cleanliness _____

Restroom cleanliness _____

Overall Impressions

Would you recommend this restaurant? _____

Opportunities for improvement _____

Mileage _____ Compensation _____ Received _____

Restaurant _____ Date of visit _____ Time _____

Server name _____ Manager on duty _____

Party member	Meal ordered	Quality	Price
		Total	

Server

Warm welcome? _____

Attentiveness and pace of service _____

Gave good recommendations? _____

Accuracy of service _____

Beverage Service

Good recommendations? _____ Checked ID? _____

Experience? _____ Quality of drinks _____

Restaurant

Restaurant cleanliness _____

Restroom cleanliness _____

Overall Impressions

Would you recommend this restaurant? _____

Opportunities for improvement _____

Mileage _____ Compensation _____ Received _____

Restaurant _____ Date of visit _____ Time _____

Server name _____ Manager on duty _____

Party member	Meal ordered	Quality	Price
		Total	

Server

Warm welcome? _____

Attentiveness and pace of service _____

Gave good recommendations? _____

Accuracy of service _____

Beverage Service

Good recommendations? _____ Checked ID? _____

Experience? _____ Quality of drinks _____

Restaurant

Restaurant cleanliness _____

Restroom cleanliness _____

Overall Impressions

Would you recommend this restaurant? _____

Opportunities for improvement _____

Mileage _____ Compensation _____ Received _____

Restaurant _____ Date of visit _____ Time _____

Server name _____ Manager on duty _____

Party member	Meal ordered	Quality	Price
		Total	

Server

Warm welcome? _____

Attentiveness and pace of service _____

Gave good recommendations? _____

Accuracy of service _____

Beverage Service

Good recommendations? _____ Checked ID? _____

Experience? _____ Quality of drinks _____

Restaurant

Restaurant cleanliness _____

Restroom cleanliness _____

Overall Impressions

Would you recommend this restaurant? _____

Opportunities for improvement _____

Mileage _____ Compensation _____ Received _____

Restaurant _____ Date of visit _____ Time _____

Server name _____ Manager on duty _____

Party member	Meal ordered	Quality	Price
		Total	

Server

Warm welcome? _____

Attentiveness and pace of service _____

Gave good recommendations? _____

Accuracy of service _____

Beverage Service

Good recommendations? _____   Checked ID? _____

Experience? _____   Quality of drinks _____

Restaurant

Restaurant cleanliness _____

Restroom cleanliness _____

Overall Impressions

Would you recommend this restaurant? _____

Opportunities for improvement _____

Mileage _____   Compensation _____   Received _____

Restaurant _____ Date of visit _____ Time _____

Server name _____ Manager on duty _____

Party member	Meal ordered	Quality	Price
		Total	

Server

Warm welcome? _____

Attentiveness and pace of service _____

Gave good recommendations? _____

Accuracy of service _____

Beverage Service

Good recommendations? _____ Checked ID? _____

Experience? _____ Quality of drinks _____

Restaurant

Restaurant cleanliness _____

Restroom cleanliness _____

Overall Impressions

Would you recommend this restaurant? _____

Opportunities for improvement _____

Mileage _____ Compensation _____ Received _____

Restaurant _____ Date of visit _____ Time _____

Server name _____ Manager on duty _____

Party member	Meal ordered	Quality	Price
		Total	

Server

Warm welcome? _____

Attentiveness and pace of service _____

Gave good recommendations? _____

Accuracy of service _____

Beverage Service

Good recommendations? _____ Checked ID? _____

Experience? _____ Quality of drinks _____

Restaurant

Restaurant cleanliness _____

Restroom cleanliness _____

Overall Impressions

Would you recommend this restaurant? _____

Opportunities for improvement _____

Mileage _____ Compensation _____ Received _____

Restaurant _____ Date of visit _____ Time _____

Server name _____ Manager on duty _____

Party member	Meal ordered	Quality	Price
		Total	

┌─ **Server** ─────────────────────────────────┐

Warm welcome? _____

Attentiveness and pace of service _____

Gave good recommendations? _____

Accuracy of service _____

└──┘

┌─ **Beverage Service** ───────────────────────┐

Good recommendations? _____ Checked ID? _____

Experience? _____ Quality of drinks _____

└──┘

┌─ **Restaurant** ─────────────────────────────┐

Restaurant cleanliness _____

Restroom cleanliness _____

└──┘

┌─ **Overall Impressions** ────────────────────┐

Would you recommend this restaurant? _____

Opportunities for improvement _____

└──┘

Mileage _____ Compensation _____ Received _____

Restaurant _____ Date of visit _____ Time _____

Server name _____ Manager on duty _____

Party member	Meal ordered	Quality	Price
		Total	

Server

Warm welcome? _____

Attentiveness and pace of service _____

Gave good recommendations? _____

Accuracy of service _____

Beverage Service

Good recommendations? _____ Checked ID? _____

Experience? _____ Quality of drinks _____

Restaurant

Restaurant cleanliness _____

Restroom cleanliness _____

Overall Impressions

Would you recommend this restaurant? _____

Opportunities for improvement _____

Mileage _____ Compensation _____ Received _____

Restaurant _____ Date of visit _____ Time _____

Server name _____ Manager on duty _____

Party member	Meal ordered	Quality	Price
		Total	

Server

Warm welcome? _____

Attentiveness and pace of service _____

Gave good recommendations? _____

Accuracy of service _____

Beverage Service

Good recommendations? _____ Checked ID? _____

Experience? _____ Quality of drinks _____

Restaurant

Restaurant cleanliness _____

Restroom cleanliness _____

Overall Impressions

Would you recommend this restaurant? _____

Opportunities for improvement _____

Mileage _____ Compensation _____ Received _____

Restaurant _____ Date of visit _____ Time _____

Server name _____ Manager on duty _____

Party member	Meal ordered	Quality	Price
		Total	

Server

Warm welcome? _____

Attentiveness and pace of service _____

Gave good recommendations? _____

Accuracy of service _____

Beverage Service

Good recommendations? _____ Checked ID? _____

Experience? _____ Quality of drinks _____

Restaurant

Restaurant cleanliness _____

Restroom cleanliness _____

Overall Impressions

Would you recommend this restaurant? _____

Opportunities for improvement _____

Mileage _____ Compensation _____ Received _____

Restaurant _____ Date of visit _____ Time _____

Server name _____ Manager on duty _____

Party member	Meal ordered	Quality	Price
	Total		

Server

Warm welcome? _____

Attentiveness and pace of service _____

Gave good recommendations? _____

Accuracy of service _____

Beverage Service

Good recommendations? _____ Checked ID? _____

Experience? _____ Quality of drinks _____

Restaurant

Restaurant cleanliness _____

Restroom cleanliness _____

Overall Impressions

Would you recommend this restaurant? _____

Opportunities for improvement _____

Mileage _____ Compensation _____ Received _____

Restaurant _____ Date of visit _____ Time _____

Server name _____ Manager on duty _____

Party member	Meal ordered	Quality	Price
		Total	

Server

Warm welcome? _____

Attentiveness and pace of service _____

Gave good recommendations? _____

Accuracy of service _____

Beverage Service

Good recommendations? _____ Checked ID? _____

Experience? _____ Quality of drinks _____

Restaurant

Restaurant cleanliness _____

Restroom cleanliness _____

Overall Impressions

Would you recommend this restaurant? _____

Opportunities for improvement _____

Mileage _____ Compensation _____ Received _____

Restaurant _____ Date of visit _____ Time _____

Server name _____ Manager on duty _____

Party member	Meal ordered	Quality	Price
		Total	

Server

Warm welcome? _____

Attentiveness and pace of service _____

Gave good recommendations? _____

Accuracy of service _____

Beverage Service

Good recommendations? _____ Checked ID? _____

Experience? _____ Quality of drinks _____

Restaurant

Restaurant cleanliness _____

Restroom cleanliness _____

Overall Impressions

Would you recommend this restaurant? _____

Opportunities for improvement _____

Mileage _____ Compensation _____ Received _____

Restaurant _____ Date of visit _____ Time _____

Server name _____ Manager on duty _____

Party member	Meal ordered	Quality	Price
		Total	

Server

Warm welcome? _____

Attentiveness and pace of service _____

Gave good recommendations? _____

Accuracy of service _____

Beverage Service

Good recommendations? _____ Checked ID? _____

Experience? _____ Quality of drinks _____

Restaurant

Restaurant cleanliness _____

Restroom cleanliness _____

Overall Impressions

Would you recommend this restaurant? _____

Opportunities for improvement _____

Mileage _____ Compensation _____ Received _____

Restaurant _____ Date of visit _____ Time _____

Server name _____ Manager on duty _____

Party member	Meal ordered	Quality	Price
		Total	

Server

Warm welcome? _____

Attentiveness and pace of service _____

Gave good recommendations? _____

Accuracy of service _____

Beverage Service

Good recommendations? _____ Checked ID? _____

Experience? _____ Quality of drinks _____

Restaurant

Restaurant cleanliness _____

Restroom cleanliness _____

Overall Impressions

Would you recommend this restaurant? _____

Opportunities for improvement _____

Mileage _____ Compensation _____ Received _____

Restaurant _____ Date of visit _____ Time _____

Server name _____ Manager on duty _____

Party member	Meal ordered	Quality	Price
		Total	

Server

Warm welcome? _____

Attentiveness and pace of service _____

Gave good recommendations? _____

Accuracy of service _____

Beverage Service

Good recommendations? _____ Checked ID? _____

Experience? _____ Quality of drinks _____

Restaurant

Restaurant cleanliness _____

Restroom cleanliness _____

Overall Impressions

Would you recommend this restaurant? _____

Opportunities for improvement _____

Mileage _____ Compensation _____ Received _____

Restaurant _____ Date of visit _____ Time _____

Server name _____ Manager on duty _____

Party member	Meal ordered	Quality	Price
		Total	

Server

Warm welcome? _____

Attentiveness and pace of service _____

Gave good recommendations? _____

Accuracy of service _____

Beverage Service

Good recommendations? _____ Checked ID? _____

Experience? _____ Quality of drinks _____

Restaurant

Restaurant cleanliness _____

Restroom cleanliness _____

Overall Impressions

Would you recommend this restaurant? _____

Opportunities for improvement _____

Mileage _____ Compensation _____ Received _____

Restaurant _____ Date of visit _____ Time _____

Server name _____ Manager on duty _____

Party member	Meal ordered	Quality	Price
		Total	

Server

Warm welcome? _____

Attentiveness and pace of service _____

Gave good recommendations? _____

Accuracy of service _____

Beverage Service

Good recommendations? _____ Checked ID? _____

Experience? _____ Quality of drinks _____

Restaurant

Restaurant cleanliness _____

Restroom cleanliness _____

Overall Impressions

Would you recommend this restaurant? _____

Opportunities for improvement _____

Mileage _____ Compensation _____ Received _____

Restaurant _____ Date of visit _____ Time _____

Server name _____ Manager on duty _____

Party member	Meal ordered	Quality	Price
		Total	

Server

Warm welcome? _____

Attentiveness and pace of service _____

Gave good recommendations? _____

Accuracy of service _____

Beverage Service

Good recommendations? _____   Checked ID? _____

Experience? _____   Quality of drinks _____

Restaurant

Restaurant cleanliness _____

Restroom cleanliness _____

Overall Impressions

Would you recommend this restaurant? _____

Opportunities for improvement _____

Mileage _____   Compensation _____   Received _____

Restaurant _____ Date of visit _____ Time _____

Server name _____ Manager on duty _____

Party member	Meal ordered	Quality	Price
		Total	

Server

Warm welcome? _____

Attentiveness and pace of service _____

Gave good recommendations? _____

Accuracy of service _____

Beverage Service

Good recommendations? _____   Checked ID? _____

Experience? _____   Quality of drinks _____

Restaurant

Restaurant cleanliness _____

Restroom cleanliness _____

Overall Impressions

Would you recommend this restaurant? _____

Opportunities for improvement _____

Mileage _____   Compensation _____   Received _____

Restaurant _____ Date of visit _____ Time _____

Server name _____ Manager on duty _____

Party member	Meal ordered	Quality	Price
		Total	

Server

Warm welcome? _____

Attentiveness and pace of service _____

Gave good recommendations? _____

Accuracy of service _____

Beverage Service

Good recommendations? _____ Checked ID? _____

Experience? _____ Quality of drinks _____

Restaurant

Restaurant cleanliness _____

Restroom cleanliness _____

Overall Impressions

Would you recommend this restaurant? _____

Opportunities for improvement _____

Mileage _____ Compensation _____ Received _____

Restaurant _____   Date of visit _____   Time _____

Server name _____   Manager on duty _____

Party member	Meal ordered	Quality	Price
		Total	

Server

Warm welcome? _____

Attentiveness and pace of service _____

Gave good recommendations? _____

Accuracy of service _____

Beverage Service

Good recommendations? _____   Checked ID? _____

Experience? _____   Quality of drinks _____

Restaurant

Restaurant cleanliness _____

Restroom cleanliness _____

Overall Impressions

Would you recommend this restaurant? _____

Opportunities for improvement _____

Mileage _____   Compensation _____   Received _____

Restaurant _____   Date of visit _____   Time _____

Server name _____   Manager on duty _____

Party member	Meal ordered	Quality	Price
		Total	

Server

Warm welcome? _____

Attentiveness and pace of service _____

Gave good recommendations? _____

Accuracy of service _____

Beverage Service

Good recommendations? _____   Checked ID? _____

Experience? _____   Quality of drinks _____

Restaurant

Restaurant cleanliness _____

Restroom cleanliness _____

Overall Impressions

Would you recommend this restaurant? _____

Opportunities for improvement _____

Mileage _____   Compensation _____   Received _____

Restaurant _____ Date of visit _____ Time _____

Server name _____ Manager on duty _____

Party member	Meal ordered	Quality	Price
		Total	

Server

Warm welcome? _____

Attentiveness and pace of service _____

Gave good recommendations? _____

Accuracy of service _____

Beverage Service

Good recommendations? _____ Checked ID? _____

Experience? _____ Quality of drinks _____

Restaurant

Restaurant cleanliness _____

Restroom cleanliness _____

Overall Impressions

Would you recommend this restaurant? _____

Opportunities for improvement _____

Mileage _____ Compensation _____ Received _____

Restaurant _____ Date of visit _____ Time _____

Server name _____ Manager on duty _____

Party member	Meal ordered	Quality	Price
		Total	

Server

Warm welcome? _____

Attentiveness and pace of service _____

Gave good recommendations? _____

Accuracy of service _____

Beverage Service

Good recommendations? _____ Checked ID? _____

Experience? _____ Quality of drinks _____

Restaurant

Restaurant cleanliness _____

Restroom cleanliness _____

Overall Impressions

Would you recommend this restaurant? _____

Opportunities for improvement _____

Mileage _____ Compensation _____ Received _____

Lightning Source UK Ltd.
Milton Keynes UK
UKHW020742140920
369879UK00015B/1861